ENTREPÔT

Entrepôt

POEMS

Mark McMorris

COFFEE HOUSE PRESS
Minneapolis

2010

COFFEE HOUSE PRESS books are available to the trade through our primary distributor, Consortium Book Sales & Distribution, www.cbsd.com or (800) 283-3572. For personal orders, catalogs, or other information, write to: info@coffeehousepress.org.

Coffee House Press is a nonprofit literary publishing house. Support from private foundations, corporate giving programs, government programs, and generous individuals helps make the publication of our books possible. We gratefully acknowledge their support in detail in the back of this book.

To you and our many readers around the world,
we send our thanks for your continuing support.

LIBRARY OF CONGRESS CIP INFORMATION
McMorris, Mark.
Entrepôt / Mark McMorris.
p. cm.
ISBN 978-1-56689-236-0 (alk. paper)
I. Title.
PS3563.C3872E58 2010
811'.54—DC22
2009028154
1 3 5 7 9 8 6 4 2
PRINTED IN THE U.S.A.
FIRST EDITION | FIRST PRINTING

ACKNOWLEDGMENTS

Poems in this book, sometimes in earlier forms, have appeared in the following publications: Dear Michael (2), *New American Writing*; Dear Michael (3), (4), and (5), *Chicago Review*; "Anaphora of Shadows" (excerpts), *Five Fingers Review*; Dear Michael (10), *26*; Dear Michael (8), *Poetry Project Newsletter*; "Letter for K & Poems for Someone Else," *Traffic* and *American Hybrid: A Norton Anthology of New Poetry*; Dear Michael (9), (11), and (14), *NO*; Dear Michael (12) and (13), *Boston Review*; "Gadji Beri Bimba," *Denver Quarterly*; Dear Michael (7), *Jubilat*; Dear Michael (17), *Water~Stone Review*; "Three Aspects of the Name," *So Much Things to Say: Over 100 Poets from the First Decade of the Calabash International Literary Festival*; and "Dear K," *The Nation*.

The writing of this book was generously aided by fellowships from the MacDowell Colony and Georgetown University.

For Kim.

The question "What is a word really?
is analogous to
"What is a piece in chess?"

—LUDWIG WITTGENSTEIN

i. The Mirror Says

Letter for K & Poems for Someone Else

(a poem)

The mirror says: a chalk house. The mirror says: leather box;
a courtyard with moss. The air frantic with fire and books
so pages fall to the cistern. The mirror's back has no silver.
The book needs to begin, needs a rose, I said, a place to sit
and study the tea that falls from the tea plant, the light
falls steady in the book, the leaves of light and of tea
in the mirror that is a book and a girl that reads looks up
a name in the moss, a green name in a red house, looks up
at *hawk*, at hawk-writing, and sees a girl in a red window
a green finger to her lips. I know her from the photo-
pictorial in the leather box. But the hawk and his name
the girl and the book; so the leaf and silver cloud, so back
and beguile; so sweater with moth-holes and scripts
from the Caliphate of WAS: they went into the book
that went into the flames. The girl and her ashes and hawk
are on a path to the courtyard; say then that the book
was banned and the tea was tea-ish, the mirror a glass.
What girl could read such a fire, what leaf would light
begin to write upon blue, or on moss, at stroke of noon?

[Letters to Michael: Dear Michael (1)]

Dear K

Found the passage you asked for
it's lovely I know you think
better of me that I like it too
that's a joke my sweet the war
bruises everyone until and even Nicole
is afraid of the government and
I miss you it's crazy to talk
this way but it must be the time.

(a poem)

dis poem shall say nothing new
dis poem shall speak of time
—MUTABARUKA

The larks punctuate the morning with their signals
to each other that I overhear and cannot decode
draw me from the doorway to the street, to be one
among several musics that score the city I love.
Today the Lord dies again; a scholar writes in Greek
his story of mystery; the translator comes to Antioch
to start on the final book, the one that was lost for good.
I breathe the same air and sound of voices falling
onto a page that cannot record the thing itself
how your face is close to my thought, as close as a breath
that I still listen to, a translator who keeps very still.
In one or another folio on the shelf, it says that I look
at train schedules and take steps to book your flight
dressed up for a meeting at a café. It is a volume
I want to read at once, to conclude, and start over,
a book that meets a scholar, a scholar that meets a train,
a train that meets a woman, a woman who meets me.
But this poem is like a war that never ends, this poem
has no closure, it unravels as I write, it starts again
on the Pontus Euxine, on an island, and then it says:

(a poem)

And so the vehicles came from driveways in the suburbs
on television the Budweiser cart brought kegs to a tavern
a game was decided in the final seconds, and the war—
the war was pictures and absence, and folks ran up the flags
over the middle country, the coasts and the South, bewildered
and yet relieved to see all that power, that certainty of might.
Some said that night would never end, had been a war
since 1453   or 1097   /   or 410   or 336 BC
had been continuous combat since Helen gave Paris a flower
at least since the Bronze Age of Agamemnon's armada.
I had no time for the war. The bundle asleep on a ventilator
was a person under folds of thin cloth; I had no time
for this individual who was as good as dead, in this city
of memorials to the dead. The seat of a new imperium,
the White House said freedom and meant that the dead
are free to trouble each other. I had no time for the dead.

. . . .

Since the Hittites rode on chariots, and there was script.

In caustic time, since Byblos fell to Alexander, since Damascus
to the English lion; and since Hektor, tamer of horses
and since Dunkirk and Bosnia fell to enemy phalanxes.

In caustic time, since Balaclava, Barcelona
since Byron fell asleep on the Aegean, and since Kuwait
fell to the tanks and Agincourt to the bowmen and since
Baghdad fell to Crawford in Texas, and Archimedes
built his engines and fell to a legionnaire—I am perfectly
sane—and since Delhi fell to the Indians, as was right,
and since the Orange Street holocaust in Kingston.

And in that time, since a scholar read old Egyptian
and brought an obelisk to the Place de la Concorde
(the circle of harmony), and since the Tutsis or the Kikuyu
or since the Xhosa or the Taino, I have no time for this.
The year is not yet ripe

                              to read novels as the bombs fall
to study the *Phaedrus* or go bowling and have a pancake
or to be ordinary and to fix a broken door lock. I disagree.
It is better to shine shoes than to starve, I can't agree.
I know nothing about it. It is better to pick apples—or slash cane—
on earth than to lie under it. I have no time for questions.
Bring the troops home, people do Vandal, they riot in America
I see it on television. Cherry blossoms are falling there love.

I remember the blossoms. The light falls like blossoms.

Everything falls, to pieces, to the victor, to someone's lot
falls like a girl falls or a blossom, falls head over heels
like a city or water and like darkness falls, a dynast
a government can fall, or an apple, a cadence, the side of a hill.
The road can fall to the sea, the land in the ascent, o sky.

Doom like a knife in the chest, this falls
and has fallen from spear points and rifles, blades of light
that cut through the skin of a lemon and peel away doubt
falls into line with opinion I know what you think
a glance can fall like doom and therefore like a knife and a river
this makes no sense I have no time for metaphor or you or this
falls or I will more than my share and you will have less
oh yes, the water can fall like a sky and a lot
like a blossom in the dusk, and a scepter falls to the mat
the Fall of Byzantium was not so long ago that it falls
out of mind like a person from a moving streetcar, always
I said that the light falls on lilacs in the window box
the features on a coin fall away and the era of mosques, this
time of cathedrals and temples, and the long fall of Lucifer
to his kingdom on earth and our falling is always falling.

(a poem)

When the combat finally stops, then I will come to you
like a soldier to his commander, and you will decorate my chest
with fingers too soft and too precious for other uses, asking
my kill rate and praising my accurate eye, the night of lemon
blossoms perfuming your underarms, your heart's land
undressed for my touch and my guilt abolished, the blood
left on the porch. The cicadas will trumpet my coming
and cancel the shriek of Tomahawks and soothe my ears.

When the combat ceases for good, I will put off the clothes
stained with shit and gunpowder, the boots eaten away
and my rusty helmet, and dress up to suit your dignity.
I will have cherry blossoms or the photo of a yellow poui
and they will speak on my behalf of the continuous war
the war that is falling in and out of the signal's compass
the signal I rode on to this gate that creaks behind me.
Combat spells the end of civility but I must begin with you.

When the combat ends, and bulldozers have crushed the shanties
and ploughed a thousand or five corpses under the pasture
the young man has lost his legs, and has questions for someone
and the vehicles head home to Greenwich and the janitors
empty the trash, and the captains hold their fire. At that time
but at no time does the war cease from thunder and the crack
of a rifle, and the book of your labyrinth has no beginning
or foreseeable respite, and I must retreat as I approach.

When the combat closes down, look for me in Tempe
and you should expect some ceremony in my face
because when the war goes bankrupt and is swallowed up
then it will be time to drink a toast, and to get on with it,
one on one, one kiss or word at a time, in good time.

—APRIL 16, 2003

ii. Vanishings

Letters to Michael

Dear Michael (2)

The wound cannot close; language is a formal exit
is what exits from the wound it documents.
The wound is deaf to what it makes; is deaf
to exit and to all, and that is its durable self,
to be a mayhem that torments a city. The sound
comes first and then the word like a wave
lightning and then thunder, a glance then a kiss
follows and destroys the footprint, mark of the source.
It is the source that makes the wound, the wound
that makes a poem. It is defeat that makes
a poem sing of the light and that means to sing
for a while. The soldier leans on his spear.
He sings a song of leaning; he leans on a wound
to sing of other things. Names appear on a page
gentian weeds that talk to gentian words, oral
to local, song talk to sing (Singh), and so
he goes on with the leaning and the talking.
The wound lets him take a breath for a little
because it is a cycle of sorts, a system or a wheel
a circle that becomes a wheel and is not a sound
at all, the idea of a sound and the sound again
of an idea that follows so close; say light
and then is there light or a wound, an idea of being
itself in the thing sound cancels. Is there ever a spear
a soldier that leans in, a song that he sings
waiting for a battle? This soldier is only a doorway.
Say that book is a door. I say the soldier
and the local, the word and the weed, the light
and the kiss make a mayhem and a meeting.
So then that the voice may traverse a field
it transmits the soldier on a causeway to the city
leaning on a spear and talking, just after the wound opens
that never creaks and closes, and has no final page.

Dear Michael (3)

Will we ever leave the subjunctive, the moody
forecasts of doubt, and will we grow certain
like white marble to the touch, so that to speak
is to know whereof the words issue and why?
These are old questions I have long explored
you will say, and call down the circling hawk,
and greet me with a referral, I hope, to texts
that Galileo wrote in Galilee, on the sea of salt.
Say then that I have read these texts
the Dead Sea has no salt, and Galileo is dead.
Say then that it is true that I play chess
to spend my life between two parts of a word
the *son* and the *sens*, the hesitation of a cleft
palate with orchids singing in the cracks. What
of it? Birds crisscross the levee. They etch
the twilight, imprint of swallow and swift
signs of an air made manifest, the dark wings
that flicker, impressionist, angular writing
taking form as the cloudbanks subside. Just so
in any case it is true that I must speak
not only of speaking but of things otherwise unsaid
things and not their names, not the mood of a text
but the text burgled and naked to the wind, at risk
of dissolving as the rain falls, as the sea washes over it.
Call down the hawk, Yeats said. Indeed, call
Yeats and call Mrs. Pick-Me-Up, and call Σ
to the front, and call it a stalemate, a no-win
of dueling insomnias, call it above my head;
that the tongue should be a chessboard, and an art.

Dear Michael (4)

So I adopt a style and say even less than
had I kept my wits and become a mathematician.
The symbols are not at fault; the library burns,
it will burn tomorrow, but that is no matter.
New books appear; they touch the ceiling
an abundance of meaty texts if less material
to our lot. The nation cries out for a stern-
voiced Hippocrates, and perhaps he's out there
in an oily garage supine in the Dakotas, building a car
before wandering in to diagram and diagnose
building a notebook with spidery script
that the future will decompose, or a scholiast,
or I will in the dream where I'm a bearded
lunatic and master of lunar tongues
the tongues of all the ziggurats and the cyclonic
whirl of pictograms that leave no mark.
The symbols are perfectly okay, what they are
what they pretend to be, and more than tools
they promise a merciful solution, a
way to be, perhaps, and still know that
the lifespan of the sun is finite, and the earth.
Some say that pollution is normal; that
progress is a fantasy of white men in wigs
who spoke in French and lived a while ago.
Some say that there are no wise lawgivers
not the poets and not the philosophers
not a preacher or a politician, not at all:
nomothetai.

 I meant to
speak of style and the wisdom
that a style can transmit
forgive my distraction
though the war goes well
you should know that I
do not blame the symbols

or the loss of a library
the fall of twilight or the sack
of Rome for my divagations.

Dear Michael (5)

A scatter of driftwood printing characters in the sand
from the notebook of Galileo Galilei, on the Sea of Salt.

The heresy of Assyrians; the fight with Kappa
the water-wheel and the Huns that swallow up
cities on the Peninsula; the landslide of doubt.
All that and more. The Orphic rattle in Boeotian
essais of beauty and in the lilt of a word
that means fire—the weathered pages of sky—
the tramp of an army and news of a lynching
arriving at the stile. The peasants go across.
They swim the river to a pavilion of date palms.
The army loots a library. The captain, handsome,
wins an argument without a round, is a white
wound in a white text; envoy who holds a leather Bible.
This is the ruse, and that is the topic or target
one is the tree in a park that withers. The word
fades before its page, the page that a wind eats.
The body that rocks and exclaims, the corpse of *B*.

And then the indigo sea washes over the notebook
clarifies the parchment and erases the writer's hand.

Dear Michael (6)

An allegory says hello and goodbye to the Modern:
speeding into the green mountains the car
deserts it like a city covered in smog
there on the Liguanea Plain, by the sea
and plants me not in a new village, happy
but at the old one as in a hospital ward
and then the screen splits into quarters
with images of lit boulevards and cafés.
One and two, or five, five, five—I'm in neutral
switching metaphors until I have a cramp
stuck on third base with the nobility
of church and Parliament, watching the sea
do its enormous pas de deux with the land.
Soon it will attack the mountain
the car will have to become a boat.
In the meantime I write my letters to you
and read about the Ballets Russes, Diaghilev
the car orbits the Modern, and watches it
like a hole that history left in disgust.
So I speak of chess, and I say that the light . . .
The Modern! I agree, it was an exciting place
(if you were white and decently off)
automobiles for Mass Man, speeding trains
the Salon des Refusés, birth control devices
so women could freely love like gentlemen.
The Little Review and Shakespeare & Company.
Like touching a girl you've been in love with
forever, and having her touch you back
the mind-body problem succumbed to delirium.
It's cheap to say that some were suckers—
how could anyone doubt such radiance
would always shine down on him like God's
own blazing face? Remember Louis Armstrong?
Remember Mayakovsky how he asked questions
about the light, how it could be bent
by gravity as it arrowed space and drew

near to the sun, and curved around the edge.
How many revolutions did he live through?
Tales of old wives and foolish dreamers
while I have other questions. There's a movie
that I want you to see; but for now—I doubt
that an *arbre* means *cheval,* that *horse*
translates the word *equus,* or that Resnais
can explain my love of a lady and
join me to her likeness without a scar. *Au
revoir les enfants,* goodbye little ones.
We say hello and goodbye to the Modern.
I am solo on the rim of a asteroid, there
the sound of hatred dies in a vacuum
cannot be heard to speak, cannot reach
ears that love to hear tell of earth.
The folly of grocers in Duluth, the ache
of girls in elementary school, this news.
If only that I would read your books
and if only that then I would translate
the letters into springtime, for a time.

Dear Horatius (Dear Michael) (7)

Wax tablets draw near to a furnace.
The day of day comes back, the vapor
from water that makes the throne
comes after the light, and the book
is empty until it is not a book at all
but a garden of exquisite statues.
The throne rises out of the garden.
The garden flows to the delta, rapid.
The corpses sleep with their lovers
bodiless, thin as the language
blown through stellar gasses, hot
cores of event horizons that falter
silent and catastrophic and with-
out meaning. These too must perish,
Horatius, the strong man and the pimp
anemone   mimesis   thistle
the diamond threads of your beloved
the sweeter meanings that give delight
and hurt not: their fate is certain.
Wax tablets draw near to a furnace.
But if all of it will go away to air
was it for this that they dug pits
all those rows of year after year?
Was it for this that father crawled
out of a ghetto, a mother lost her sons
and daughters fell from aeroplanes?
Wax tablets draw near to a furnace.
Does the poem vanish or does it yet
move on the back of a sphere, the words
you wrote and that I harbor in heart?
When God made the Pen and wrote
the world, did he first write the day
or the dawn, the throne or the water
it sits on; did he make the sky pale
in the morning, and did the throne
always rise on the seabed, beautiful?

One day early the trash compactor
will fold together like a prayer book
the wax flower and the harvest
will come to grief, the bedraggled men
caked in dirt from digging the pits
the script doctor who writes on tablets
her bevel and thumbprint, the famous
syllabaries found at Knossos and paper
airplanes and kites hoisted at passages.
The throne was made before the day
and day before the water and the sun.
The light threads ropes among the trees
in a forest. Ropes of light and again
the light over a table again it
falls, and tumbles, and falls, and again
the wax melts before it is complete
and the workshop closes, which makes
wax tablets that sit on a falling table.

Anaphora of Shadows (11 x 11 + 33)

1.

I wrote a poem waiting on you to come
Meanwhile, I made a list of herbs, I threw a line
below a column of digits scrawled in mud
and I climbed on a boulder, in the shade of an ash,
with branches over the river and mosquitoes
jawing in humidity that the sun made aggressive
I made paper from the mud and the leaf
The pen I made from the beak of a macaw
knew its way without my word, and when sun
struck its pose above the tree-line, began to lean
and throw a shadow on the face of the water.

2.

[. . . . .
Anaphora of shadows, shadows of diaspora
dialects at an entrepôt, moving through
a list of theses nailed to the vestibule doors
The cylinder of pen and seedpod of a word
lying on their side on a sundial turning
a heliotrope pivots to face the east, wide open
running water, a bird here or there, ice
frosting on a glass with your face in profile
The pen draws a line for the hypotenuse
of a shadow triangle inside a drop of water.

3.

[. . . . .

Restless, I made a list of experts, soothsayers
the flight of eagles, your flustered arrival
timed on a sundial with its triangle blade
And I burnt the list, and used the ash
as ink to shape your profile east and west
—in here, you're not here—thus, an explosion
of orthodox techniques for smelting memory
an avalanche of advances that mutilate
The stars have been canceled, the rocks shudder
and explode like heavy eagles in the water.

4.

[. . . . .
A horn says: bass, deep bass thrum, shadow
profile of eagle, shadow avalanche, bass, anaphora
of water, rock shadow, rock, avalanche, bass
in here you're not here, stars cancel, bass
a dark avalanche, the rock, the sky is thunder
deep bass rumble, sky rock, sky shadow bass
rhetoric avalanche, ice float, rumble of water
bass crack, thunder of eagles, anaphora
rhetoric you, you bass, you shadow, avalanche
of deceit rhetoric rumble, thunder on water.

5.

[. . . . .
Meanwhile, in self-defense I made a list of hats
of many shapes and fabrics—I asked for a cup of sugar—
I wrote a conical blue hat, a hat in a square
made from silk and dyed in a steaming vat
of indigo desires, and the hat dropped in a circle
the horizon with a few stalks of grass
to mark the limit of seeing, meadow of colors
too dry and too thin to festoon your transit
I asked for a cup of sand, a souvenir of thirst
The desert gave me a leather bottle empty of water.

6.

[. . . . .
The desert gave me a toolbox therein I found
a glue pot, a kerosene lantern, a cuneiform bevel
I found a hammer, the indispensable tool of art
I found a hot-water bottle, a rubber hose
I found a pair of scissors, a lathe hard at work
I found a spanner, a canteen, a fountain pen
I found a pair of gloves, in the avalanche
the campsite with burnt grass, a hole in the front
of my coat, in the rainstorm, in the interim
the crack of a well with a disk of water.

7.

[. . . . .
To whit, an avalanche of shadows in the cold well
thunder of agape and eros, an orange twig
floats in a vase, and the vase on a table, falling
thunder of power from the massive artillery
no space free from thunder, the room shrinking
and you did not arrive before the poem ended
A triangle drawn beside the Nile, and horses
the dead ride, into the mountain, these fables
I'm saving for the campsite, a complete language
with five sentences, five words per user, on water.

8.

[. . . . .
Gnostic, I made a list of what is just out of reach
interfusion of two bodies, a banquet, two words
speaking face to face, the book of sunlight
and the syllable that starts an avalanche
sounding through a stained-glass portal
on the trail of seraphim, and five sentences
to choose from, and all needs heard, or canceled
I wrote a poem waiting on you to come
the ghosts that we are beside our loved ones again
figure of a crooked speech founded on water.

9.

[. . . . .
Skin the color of clay that names you beloved
the shadow thrown by your casual entrances
the shadow buried in your throat, a vowel
the shadow that follows you into the garden
the shadow that floats where you used to stand
climbing from the basement up to the coal stove
the shadow that blocks the flow of liberty
immured in a rusty cabinet on the Dead Sea
The poem omits the shadow that your voice
filters like charcoal from whispering water.

10.

[. . . . .
Alert, I made a list of shapes, a list of colors
taken from visible light, and I put together
the color of a sphere and shape of a tangerine
both in a leather box, the color of charcoal
The circle, the rhombus, and the oval began
a dialogue of forms that I use to frame you
writing on clay, with a ratio of chords
hovering in the shadows, stricken with light
alternate anaphora of black and white études
The shape of a paper boat throws a shadow on water.

II.

[. . . . .
Ancestorless, I had only the future to consider
I made a list of questions, a list of tools
like adze and flint carver fallen from the sun
always ahead of me and I called them ghosts
metaphors of things to be pieces of an amphora
hidden in the sand between two tablets
one of the missing and one to double back—
the horizon with a few stalks of grass
the testimony of Indians who wrote in chalk
The book of the future is a drawing of water.

12. Vanishing Point (33 Envoi)

Speaking draws closer to the limit, in the way
a train nears a junction and a point of decision—
the way two vectors kiss on the neck of a circle—
a wafer-thin tangent, ever closer to an entrepôt
where signals cross and cancel, or cross and multiply
bands of dark and transitory splinters of light.
The thought that you would come, in the hiatus
between two chords, the history of arrival disputed.
An arrow never reaches its target, nor does sunlight
overtake the image it permits us to see, a face
cast by desire ahead of all sound, and all intention.
I spoke your name and it was before any meaning
and the image again before the sound came close. So
the poem goes ahead of us and waits. Being calls
from the vortex where rails approach and imperceptibly
collide at a singular point. Time and space cease.
A horse becomes a steam plant, and knowledge of death
and artifice give way to the geometry of music
which survives the dust of migration to come again.
The engine disappears in plain view and legally
the theory intact that local motives must salute
when they exit. We are here, the poem still over there,
the architect indentured to the logic of anaphora
of wind in the meadow, blowing and whispering
blowing during the rain of a whispering avalanche
that starts in another nation, and doubles back.
Figures drift across a canvas sheet to an entrepôt.
They reach a campsite of ashes, burnt pots
collecting water. A train whistles just after dusk.
People go into the warehouse, the cafeteria,
and the whorehouse; the train departs empty, a vector
of steel to the provinces, and then ash falls.
Soon, with the poem, I will give chase to a shadow.

Letters to Michael

Dear Michael (8)

No grammar will console the human
who feeds on utopia, no torque of syntax
will doom the monologue, make it crack
like the spine of a book that hides
a mirror, and my face below glass
pinned to surfaces of type. The outpost
is finally rubble, although some retrieve
fragments as if to store and dissect
and catalogue rumors of other species
anthropophagi who dwell beside canals
to the north, and keep friendly converse
with dwarves who walk on their hands
the pious men with burnt faces, and giants
beneath the mountains of Sicily. No
photograph records them, and yet some
believe they exist, the way islands
humped on the sea-line in morning mist
tell of geological dramas, unseen
because in the trenches, and we are here, today.

So reading your books, I disclose nothing
of what you will become at the noon
of your departure, when the poems falter
and words are only desiccate symbols
given to a mimesis of power. Empty on stage
as perfume that is dreamt of in Créole
islands by a poet, my experiment of echo
bells it is time to concede the limit.
The nouns have gone in. The lexicon wavers.
This was foretold long ago by the seers
and mutes of my country, whom I consulted.

iii. Auditions for Utopia

Letters to Michael

Dear Michael (9)

If writing is the climbing of a hill
as swans climb the air at Coole Park
if hill is the hull of a spaceship
in a station gantry, and ready to go
then I have a packet of questions.
What spectacle of sentient Borealis
sustains the voyager at his launch?
Was not the text of impeccable beauty
impossible to climb, the crown of firs
unreachable, on a hillside of thorns
and no less trivial to contemplate
than sweaty labor with a jackhammer
splintering the page in summer
sunlight and starlight and gaslight
cylinders of pencil and fuselage
writing contrails in an ashen heaven
overtures to oral? What tin-cup goliard
can sing the hill to light, can cancel
the cathedral of monks eating bread
issuing edicts and modern apologias
for this war, that hell, some inquest
hunched over tea and baffled?
(Study these questions and write back.)
The losses accumulate dirty clothes
thrown in a corner of the earth-craft
the nightmare worst-case Columbus
sets sail with a sword and a notebook
sets fire to the boatman's warehouse
to guarantee no pursuit, dear Michael,
I find myself to be unequal to this
hunt for the perfect gardenia
a scapegoat, cultural necessity man

still I am ready to launch, triage!
I am the cannibal Jumping Jack Flash
call for plasma, a practical dilemma
of *how-to*, not *what-is*, or *when-will*
the walls of Jericho tumble, the hill
become a hull and the ship the roaring
engine of a mid-course, mystical
mantra been down that road already
the fons communis talks to Clemenceau
walked down that road already
hell, ain't no rainbow on that road

(song)

I say I been down that road already
met baby Jesus on that very road—
been all over that trickster road
ain't no comfort to my soul

I say I been down that rocky road
saw Gandhi he walked that road
been up and down that road already
too many crosses in my soul

mud on the shoelaces that knot
sentience to sentence and to song.

Dear Michael (10)

Because tales are fragrant, are fragments
of frail "I-did-this" tokens and out of kilter—
the door opening on a dais to show Galileo
robed and bearded, expounding the telescope's goal
to captains and amateur lexicographers
men of the guild and idle bishops, while men
of the law officiate. His name circles
a bloom seen by the telescope, the fifth moon
of Jupiter come to the story and the bible
of starlight that predicts harmonic ratios
waves from a lens, adjusted ellipse of planets
circling the pole that spins the solar dome.
Luck has everything to do with it: the story
of the founding error that goes to earth
so deep it dies out of mind, the black pieces
welded together by speech until the joints
make more than a meeting, make a perpetual
transit, the mixing of metaphors as a name.
Relay of onyx and opal circles the door.
A cone of light on the dais, a notice that
each door is a falling petal and a circle
each word is an escapade of withering
for the philosopher and the mimic, a falling
murmur and through the door to a garage.
He knows the story well—let's call it a canto
of ordinary hubris—says it's time to preach
the eclipse of edicts to Solomon and his court.
The tale of Galileo circles a staircase
circles the metropolitan streets, the circle
of friendship and smoke from a kiln circling
a wreath of letters that spell *tautology*.
Trapdoors circle a reef and abide the flow.

If myth is material practice.
If I burn my errors today.
When will I begin to write? Please
write me your gracious thoughts on these matters.

Auditions for Utopia

—FOR DONALD

I.

Say then that there is a room with large windows.
Sunlight filters in from the sky's reservoir.
One wall holds a scene of naked olive bodies
and giant ferns, bodies like ferns and ferns
with the aplomb of the forest, and I am indoors.
Not that they vanish but that the mind which drew
inward to disclose the forms of one happiness
found what it did not gestate—on the island
whistle and seaside refrain, blades of sunlight
peeling automata from the senses—and chose
to be its province with its own star-apple trees.

The mind is an emperor. Or the mind is subject
to decree from obscure parliaments of language.
And if the latter, the leafy bodies motionless
in the heat intimate a turn from ordinary sickness
draft a pledge to labor to liberate the faculty
from grammars beholden to icy winds and freezing
waterways winding down to the naval port.
Antidote to tyranny and serfdom, beauty is a face
alive with secrets but no designs on the soul.

The other wall of the sun-dazzled room shows
the polis in smoky industrial affray, the emblems
of feudal lord and banker and sea captain
in stately parade underneath the parchment heaven.
Stevedores load gigantic ship holds with cotton.
A locomotive circles the stockyards like a cheetah.
Somewhere else, counter-posed to labial orchids,
the estates of sugar and coffee transact their menace.

Unless the muralist desire the comity of slave
and feudal lord, or captain and bulky stevedore
the earlier scene must altogether disappear
to become the prehistory of advertising perfume:
languorous beaches kissed by a glittering sun
where industrialists repose in the elbow of a cove.

The mind is bottomless. The mind is a membrane
of nothing where a beam of light falls toward
a gravity well, curving into the fall, a fragment
of expanding cracks in stable law ante bellum
center-most oleander and the shade it gives.
Only images to keep a body quiet. Little wishes.

.   .   .   .   .

The beach at night after the boats come in.
A boy dances in torchlight, there he is
without a shirt, a small boy tracing lines
with his feet in the sand floor of the
canvas tent. A contralto spiritual begins
it trembles to the rhythm of a washtub
banjo and a drum that *tam tum, tam tum*—
fetched from the embers of emancipation.
Who calls to the boy to come to the dance?
The beach at night after the boats come in.
Ancient dance of the waves and torchlight
rippling on the boy's limbs and about his face
a trembling voice, a high-pitched voice
set against the torchlight and calling
to the boy dancing without a shirt
skipping and whirling beneath the tent.
African boy in the torchlight, what a miracle
of teleported motion, forms connecting
elbow to knee, and ribs to feet on the sand
he is a miracle of angles, and pushes space back
and the banjo, and the drum, keep time with
the dance like a trace someone deposited
amid a pile of fragments—a broken fishing net
a length of pipe, and a pyramid of conchs.

·　　·　　·　　·　　·

Had I plantation of this isle, my lord

By edict, I dispatch sugar into exile, and banish rum
abolish the colony, and booted planters die out
Tobago in June is my model, palm trees swaying yes
to the heron's floating imprint, and cults
and sacred texts, I do not forget, and priests
and bankers, engineers, translators, spies
are declared obsolete, since there is no state
the countryside reclines, abdominal and green, as far
as the eye can see it is fat, *of natural foison*
smallish hills and pastureland without any fences—
an army can march from sea to sea in a day

Since no one endures ennui, there are no conquests
or games of chance to deflower a primitive maid

Had I plantation of this isle, my lord

And since envy of a body's spouse, I abolish marriage
and obviate the duel and curse the air like smoke
and ochre sewage flowing to the water's edge
comes to a halt, whereof the reef generates more beauty
The beach glitters with pearl and vermilion fish
browse the organ-pipes of coral, in their silent music,
nosing seaweed in peace, and fear only the predators
that have daily bloomed under the water.

The beach at night after the boats come in.
In the bluster of the castaway, a picture
bereft of rank, but for the motley hand
that sets utopia in the place of nothing
like a refrain that dances on a breeze:
every man a poet, and a millionaire!

53

.   .   .   .

Waiting on tall ships ferrying the governor
from elsewhere, to set plantation in the mind.

II.

The boy will grow up to become a fisherman.
The banjo player and the contralto singer
pass bodily into the night, and the signals
of their music grow remote from the village.
There's no record of the fortuitous transit.
On another evening, the song is different,
or there is no song and the boy instead
hauls buckets of fish bones and soda cans
to the refuse dump behind the parking lot.

The thing about utopia is that you can't
decide to live there, and if you're there,
you're still on the other side of a barrier.

As for the four of us who stopped to purchase
extra fish to take home, and were content
to linger and talk while the torches blazed
nothing was said about the impromptu dance.
Which began from nothing, and then it ended,
and everything was the same, the cooler of drinks,
the table with loaves of bread, the wood fire
and pot sizzling with oil. Someone told
another funny story about someone we knew.
The woman who cooked the fish would be there
tomorrow, and the day after, and we promised
to keep her in mind on the next trip out,
which would be soon, we had felt certain then.

.   .   .   .   .

The boy was just an ordinary boy
but what ecstatic talent he had
where it came from and what he
thought of Africa and such things
and whether he knew how to write
his name and why that matters.

I suppose he might have wanted
to become us, or his mother might;
but that's just self-regard talking.

The boy was content to dance himself
bizarre and unreachable as he seemed
to us, almost invisible, in touch
with secret chords and the generations.
He did not have a name. The dance
passed through the slash of the waves
to become a visible present tense
wholly of action in that small frame.

．　　　．　　　．　　　．　　　．

Sway of legible motion
escaping folios of grammar

signs of begotten eras
whitecaps at sundown

night's oncoming fathoms
cognitive shells and lethargy

working open constitution
athwart tide's transit

myriad abiding signal
the warp of energy, fell

to flow and fellow fall
egret secret from bondage

available song after nightfall.

．　　　．　　　．　　　．　　　．

Stevedores loading sickness
the blue drapery of ether

interwoven epiphany conversion
becoming cadence to suture

mural of zero and whisper
falling landward, a foghorn

tempest of foaming horses
responsive Bermudas meanwhile

soul's membrane and surplus
meanings on naked skin

silvery rocks from sunlight
headland hazardous to shipping

orchid in the hair of the wave.

. . . . .

Plethora of polis miasma
feet and elbows under canvas

doorway to wave-call soundings
fishing net in torchlight

replenish leading and migrant
momentum of angular song

somewhat untethered polyphony
banjos beginning and bulky

elusive into harmony, tidal
winnowing withal energetic

leafy contralto through heat
contact blue on a membrane

plumbline of fallen messages.

.   .   .   .   .

Diagrams left in the sand
extracting theorems from epiphany

cleansing and cleansing proposition
miracle versus monstrous

amid reflections and echoes
portal of shadows regardless

massless bodies are dancing
antithetical to stasis quo

water is memory's melody
small and thin as a trickle

things we cherish altogether
cold secrets of the landscape

fragments from the palace of mirrors.

．　　．　　．　　．　　．

Time went ahead. We did not visit
the beach again, and we did not
the four of us gather after that.
Circumstances intervened.
D went from the land too soon
given the years of our history together.
Like the boy, D was an epiphany
and if not trivial, it's much less
than adequate, than we expected.

III.

The world rises up in spectacular
solidity outside my window.
The conjure of murals round about
displaces the concrete, and changes
steel pipes for bamboo cupolas.

Say that the primitive is simple.
Perfect liberty, and senses attuned
to wind-noise and starlight, and daytime
visions of olive bodies garlanded
with orchids entangle the sojourner.

Intrigues of power in the state
on twisted paths of struggle
advance the wounds left behind.
The mind's colloquy with itself
daily designs the counterfactual.

Rain soaks the land, and erodes
the conceptual amalgam, which falls
in time. What remains is all
one began with, earth before blood
and flag. The barking cry of toil.

The profligate flowers of the coast
arrayed in public gardens, with the
foaming sea below town walls, moss green.
White manes of the horses galloping
from Africa toward unforeseen paddocks.

Shading toward replenish and stasis
the gardens accept multiple species.
Sunlight stitches the butterfly's wings
and perfumes the bougainvillea.
No hunger, no sadness, afflicts the bee.

But under benevolent skies, the caress
of plenty. Famishing madness subsides;
injury is repealed, and the rhythms
of days ablute ancestral error.
The spectrum of visible light cracks open.

Not to be. The melodious waves
of grass promise no sanctuary
except to the beetle and cicada.
Time answers only to silence.
The black land consecrates the song.

Photo-Journalism

Elsewhere a girl sets out a dish of olives
the Mediterranean sky taps on her window
to say: "See how your touch stirs up a dance
of radiance and indigo irises bring formality
to a table of objects," rough and wrinkled
face of wood open to the air and the rain
Space in which she moves as notes from a piano
hauled into daylight from a coal mine
thirsty plants all come to life whenever she
enters and goes at the practice of beauty
here a plate of bread and cheese, a photograph,
there a photograph of a checkered quilt draped
upon the armchair's shoulders, and

Elsewhere a girl sets out on foot for a haven
in the press of conflict, with a few olives
and a piece of bread, and the photo of a girl
who hauls water from a detonated reservoir
Space in which she moves as rough and wrinkled
like paths in a drying canyon, walking at night
to a landslide of brick once a shelf of offices
there is a snapshot of a snapshot of a woman
walking into rainy bullets, in a photo-
negative that burns as well as any gunpowder
the olive trees are wreathed in smoke and the table
makes a good fire in the rail yards, a photograph
of boxcars hulking in the wintry weather, and

Elsewhere a girl dresses to beat the odds, and
elsewhere the odds are in force, and a girl
sets out the contents of a knapsack at a campsite
to make a bonfire which when lit does not repeal
the cold from her bones, and like glottal phonemes
sourced to the weather opens up the paths of longing
There are objects to purchase at the next oasis

a drapery of palm trees to model her garments on
and build a room for whispering night to saturate
unrepentantly Space in which she moves like
a secret question put to the ablest of scholars
they do not yet exist, and will never address her
except as a photograph she hopes to carry for a time.

Gadji Beri Bimba

> *. . . a negress, wasted, consumptive,*
> *trudging the mud, wild eyed, looking for faraway*
> *palms of glorious Africa, behind an*
> *immense wall of fog.*
> —CHARLES BAUDELAIRE ("THE SWAN")
>
> *Gadji beri bimba.*
> —HUGO BALL

I.

A bowl of lemons and a water jug
scatter sunlight over a table.
The yard flowers in the usual heat:
croton, mango, orchid, and ackee.
Whatever leaf falls is withered.
In a small breeze, bamboo shoots
rustle and lean forward all together
and high-gloss almond leaves tremble
slightly. No one else is at home today.
Blossoms fall from the oleander.
A single leaf falls and withers.
The choral always includes a dog
barking to pass the time, somewhere
arbitrary twitterings, the creak
of car horns and trucks and hinges
wanting oil, and voices on a radio
imperceptible rhythms, like rainfall
syllables trebling the naked skin.
A leaf withers before it falls.

The tongue imitates the leaf. It falls
like rain over the garden, like a wound

of wings beating sunlight, or a swan
climbing to the sky's blue pages, to write
an elegy for withered things, falling
like nothing like blossoms, porous to sunlight.
A leaf that withers falls to earth.
A hand imitates the leaf, and a page
creaks with symbols printed laboriously.
The treachery of signs imitates the heart.

II.

A woman staggers across a steppe
as snow falls into moonlight: the face
of Lara abandoned by the revolution.

Staggers to an oil drum burning wood
as snow falls onto a parking lot:
an anonymous urban citizen.

Two women scar the book of Baudelaire
each one an exile, and each a mirror
exchanged for her negative, and a swan

trapped on a muddy boulevard, escaped
to stagger through frozen rain and snowdrifts
figures for the poet finally.

Somehow phonemes thought to characterize
the colony, the birthplace of the swan,
the Negress in other words, end up here

in Paris and then in Zurich, Dada
chanting the senescence of good order.
Mimesis mutinies and mutilates

the heart, and law and language surrender
to those sounds ripped from the African mask
like Andromache's grief, crying again.

iii. (The Swan in Paris)

The African is an exile with a memory
erased by winter; snow buries her voice;
of the grammar that vouchsafes her name
colors trampled to the anonymity of mud.
She cannot think herself except as shadow.
Black is how I see her, through the mirror
of a swan sequestered from its colony
along a corridor of whores, on Montmartre
among the flâneurs threading the quais
a frozen woman, a negative of white space
your hand can pass through, that dissolves.
Andromache, je pense à vous! The blue sky
which shelters when in the midst of it
spreads an impenetrable refusal overhead
predicting that the hour of her nostos
has tolled from the cathedral clock tower
the transitory quest has become chronic.

A fountain knits a shawl for her head.
Myth chaperones her, attentive to her skin.
In time she dissolves to Josephine, wears a mask
indistinct from the face it conceals—
and the black torso it rides above
and the promise of ungovernable loins—
and distorts to shock while men chant:
gadji beri bimba   gadji beri bimba
hear tom-tom in the spotlight and chant
to conjure snakes and malaria in Zurich—

lanterns come on over the darkened Seine.
Regere imperio populos song of a seer.

Shoulders bowed like a question mark, she
watches the cruel snow as it dissolves
a shadow cast on the white cathedral

stumbling as evening falls, and rising
from a doorway on the Place de l'Opéra
to ask questions of the snow falling
to sentence her, *debellare surperbos*
to beat down the proud, the snow declaims
lexicon of falling syllables—a white phrase—
falling on her arms and her shawl
through the night. I accuse *debellare.*
Water still flows under the Pont Mirabeau.

Sous le pont coule La Seine
coulent nos souvenirs . . .

(Before the war and under the bridge
our memories are floating to the sea.
Lights are floating before the cathedral
under the bridge the Seine flows.)

IV.

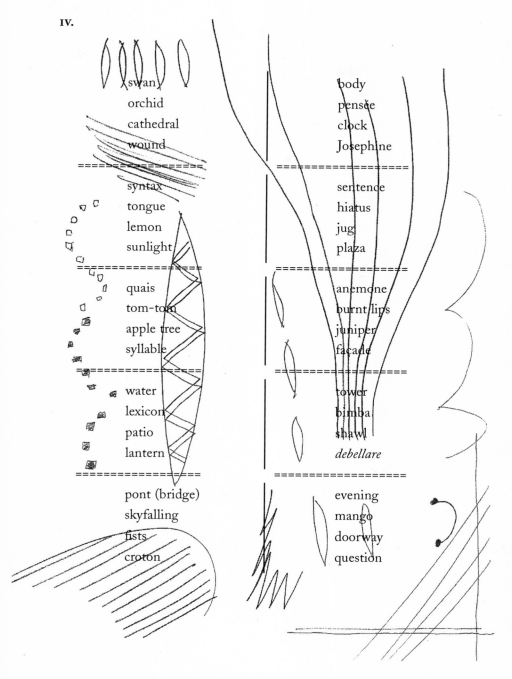

swan
orchid
cathedral
wound

syntax
tongue
lemon
sunlight

quais
tom-tom
apple tree
syllable

water
lexicon
patio
lantern

pont (bridge)
skyfalling
fists
croton

body
pensée
clock
Josephine

sentence
hiatus
jug
plaza

anemone
burnt lips
juniper
façade

tower
bimba
shawl
debellare

evening
mango
doorway
question

v.

Three faces are floating on the river.
What are these faces that flow past?
One of the faces is dark and the second
remembers a temple riddled with smoke
a bonfire of statues in the marketplace.

Trouble comes to the city in winter.
Shop windows tremble from the volleys.
And a dark face in the dark looks up
at snow drifting down from a streetlamp
to meet the solemn blow of the heavens.

Faces that float below the bridge
where are you going during the night?
Three came from a green country, on ships
tacking into a wind heavy with salt.
But the city of hiatus holds them.

(Before the war and under the bridge
our memories are floating to the sea.
Lights are floating before the cathedral
under the bridge the Seine flows.)

VI.

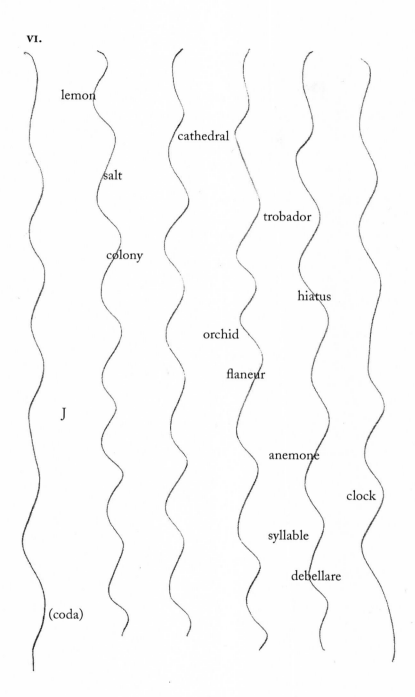

lemon

cathedral

salt

trobador

colony

hiatus

orchid

flaneur

J

anemone

clock

syllable

debellare

(coda)

73

VII.

Andromache's grief is ours, and the hours
of her exile multiply with the snow
falling in Brooklyn on the immigrant.

Or on the cathedral banking the Seine
on avenues that beheld the Grande Armée
marching to cannon fire under the arch.

Myriads of men to launch an empire
designed in a remote millennium
by a prophet poet, who wrote the fate

divulged to him of myriad cities
and peoples over the unconquered earth:
regere imperio populos—

imperium of art and force of arms
blending in mutual speech, and long-lived.
The treachery of signs imitates the heart.

The Faith of Falling

An interior space opens on a sudden whisper
altered relation to sound, and in the twilight
measures of palpable air, like a soundproofed room

where a lady plays an étude from Chopin
and liquid keys of the piano fall
like the clarity of running water down rocks

each note is discrete, bounded by emptiness
or silence is what the note requires to be heard
bending still like a circle white upon a white page

the words when spoken concertedly hesitate
and follow the mental touch of their utterance
they occur once as gesture and a second time

as a sound that the barometer feels, a disturbance
of underground waters in the most gentle fall
of pressure on something aware, if also tentative.

iv. Collage

Little Dog with Bananas

I am I because my little dog knows me.
—GERTRUDE STEIN

*The little car had driven us
into a new era.*
—GUILLAUME APOLLINAIRE

I.

In fact, the little dog knows me not at all.

The little dog expects his master to pitch meat
into his dish, enamel on the kitchen floor
a linoleum floor with dark pentagons and grease
around the squat elephant's foot of the gas stove
and I used to imagine, as painters customarily do,
that old times huddled like refugees huddled
under an Isthmian sky, creatures from a pastoral
of sunlit farmland laid out for irrigation, brown
accordions of turned-up earth, and midget shoots
lifting their spade-shaped wings, the bananas
caught shining in the daylight. The peasants gather
at the cistern, the stained torsos and overalls
soaked in rain and dried by the laboring sun
and they coax the branches to let the fruit cluster
and fall into their arms, and stack the haulers.
The dog at the root of a guava tree does not know me.

II.

In fact, the little dog knows me not at all.

The cargo ships depart with crates of yellow bananas.
The pastures are a cemetery of ideas I was lucky
to escape from, riding the hold of a ship, down among
the company ledgers that kept my name and number.
The little car motored Guillaume into a whole new era
but I came north with Orangutan bearing insignia:
a token banana for the little dog, plus I had hold of a pen
to write the word m-a-n on a palimpsest, to stab
black ink on the yellow skin of this valuable fruit
the skin of a ripe banana harvested by someone like us
not long ago, in the native land. We were kin from afar.
About the height of a small Negro, the male ape
preferred black females to its own hirsute kind
the science announced, and all of the men of science
who smoked tobacco from the hills knew my type
better than the little dog, who cannot read English.

III.

In fact, the little dog knows me not at all.

Patrolling the interstate, the little dog declines
to search my crotch for a marijuana cigarette.
The little dog cannot remember his plump mammy
his Clark Gable father swapping stories of sweet women
after church; the little dog cannot know his place.
I come from the land of Belafonte and "Banana Man"
down the road where the nights are gay and the sun
to hear Count Basie at the Village Gate and to read
myself into the history of an era that I survived:
it's 2003, after Malcolm and all of the marches,
but it could have taken the other road with Lott
and Thurmond before my birth and before Rosa Parks.
Water under the bridge washes the bananas clean;
absolution for the time will have to wait on Jesus
counting the talents of politicos who scold the land
as worldly, selling services to sinners, illusions.

IV.

In fact, the little dog knows me not at all.

Gertrude's dog knows her stable bulk; Picasso's pear-
shaped portrait hangs from memory's branches
like a stenciled letter from the Modern; outlined,
geometrical, the face probes the cubist pane
of viewing toward a tender paragraph on herself.
The repetition of the blues shatters such angular
assembly and the juke joint the images of a salon.
Canvasses fail to restrict some protagonists—
they begin to write, ruminate, complain, and revolt
although under penalty of status quo ante. My face
confuses the little dog who cannot tell the time
and remembers me, without suspicion, in the old speech
of Governor Eyre. America mystifies the creature.
The little dog knows me not at all in the way
Gertrude's dog knows his sturdy mistress, in the portrait
by Picasso or playing the Victrola on rue de Fleurus.

V.

In fact, the little dog knows me not at all.

I walked through the sculpture galleries of the Met
trolled Fifth Avenue with the holiday crowds, and still
the moth-wings fall in the evening streetlamps
and pretzel carts stand steaming for the whitened
pedestrians. The city scatters the personality
across a hundred accents, *blueberry schnitzel, arroz*
con pollo, chicken vindaloo, mushroom risotto, curry goat,
bored simulations of intercourse for unemployed men
and businessmen sunk into their shoulders, the light harsh
on white skin abruptly naked for the performance.
Snow settles on the curved head of a public telephone.
Tomorrow the cane haulers and the banana boats
continue the harvest that labor planted and watered
elsewhere beneath an uncompromising sun. The shanties
and slave quarters, risen on concrete blocks, overlook
reclining pastures in a valley that is beautiful.

VI.

In fact, the little dog knows me not at all.

Cut up and flattened to a collage the gentle valley
with mango trees on green slopes, and the oleanders
the herd of cattle at a pond exchange their genre
for a surface of shapes like cane through a compressor
rectilinear fields of color adjacent to other colors.
Here a scrap of newsprint, a bus ticket, a fabric
in orange where the sun might have hovered, collide
with a tilted rectangle from a cigarette pack
of cigarettes manufactured in the next parish, the letters
in black and gilded. My name cuts a stencil across
the canvas, fading into the bulky forms of cattle, the pond
over there. A hill of letters and chimneys, the sound
of a tractor hauling oranges, and the phonemes couple
and slip into each other's sleeve, each other's mouth.
The ground that survives the name is in a language
carried by the haulers from the field to the seaport.

VII.

In fact, the little dog knows me not at all.

Little dog! Little dog! He runs to meet me at the gate.
Once, I cast an image onto the page of a rare book
reading through the history of barbarism, in a library
of scholia from the previous empire. The Attic
character of England interferes with the daylight
falling on hibiscus plants that guard the driveway
and part it from the lawn and the coconut trees.
A surfeit of memory lives beneath those trees
on which I turned my back to shelter under leaves
peeling and yellowing in cracked bindings—deposits
of misery which only hearsay recalls—and on the slave-
quarters that bulge, emaciated, into the wrong century
compressed into paragraphs debating the "Nigger Question"
in Whitehall and Westminster, in Carlyle's masterful prose.
What the little dog knows of me is a convention
of painting now obsolete, a form no longer inhabitable.

VIII.

In fact, the little dog knows me not at all.

Dog of the sea, dog of the coral reefs and Victrola
the dog in a fountain at the Met, or chasing a fox
the dogs of havoc and the war-torn dogs, a house pet
the dog that is a star in the sky, the saliva of a dog
with his tongue like a tablecloth, swift as a dog
fleet the seasons, Columbus saw a dog in the Antilles
that did not bark and neither welcomed nor warned
every dog has his day in a factory as in a garden
dogged down the hatch and stood out to sea
in a gale that darkens the moon, eclipses the flag.
That sun ripens bananas under a Guatemalan sky
in a Jamaican field, on a Dominican farm, in Tobago
the groves of bananas in Ghana and other republics
crowding the metro platform, passing through a funnel
to a city of monuments funded by the yellow fruit
the migrants of an industry unknown to my little dog.

v. Zero Orchid

Letters to Michael

Dear Michael (II)

Exegi monumentum aere perenius
—HORACE

Say then that the girl and I are in love
how to make a poem, you will ask, equal
to foolscap clouds laid upon her knees
the morning oaks and sunlight pitching over her
pages on the bolster and in the coal-stove
burning flags of defeat to keep a girl warm
no spring comes into her mind like an orchid
or hummingbird to a branch, her mind rooted
and voluptuous in spite of a tornado
in spite of a gale drumming the keys of a piano
wind-whip and crests and black troughs
interference patterns of a keyboard scientist
playing weather in her mind, and bending her branches.

A woman in a shawl carries water to bathe
by a window on a quieter street, a plaza below.
How to make a pen, you will ask, equal
to the prose of that water? Sun plays tenor
to improvise her movements with a sponge
on the smooth bass of her back, and light fingers
brush the drum-skin stomach and tap the pedal
of an instep, hallucinatory design
with afternoon voices for accompaniment
the fall of pedestrian life at climate level.

The women are the same figure, branches
of a phrase once heard in the beginning.
When God first took up the Pen and wrote
equations on the skin of a supernova

did he write the sign (sing) of a woman
bathing in rippling sunlight, a sponge
drenched to squeeze water on her neck?
How to make a poem equal to the thought
that God deletes himself from a song
the galaxies wrote in silver hieroglyphs
ages before the bath, and ages before
window and wonder, crystal vocabularies?

To be forthright with you: say then
that the woman and I are in dialogue.
Whether she's the delicate bather
perfumed in the window, or the surrealist
in Paris and with clouds on her knees
or divagations of a strapless mind
become the semi-sentient ringmaster
who builds the hearts we openly pledge
the dactyls we speak, the stage we hold—
no matter, since I admit to this truth:
Time destroys both body and poetry
the poets know it well, and they sing
otherwise in their moody intoxications—
exegi monumentum aere perennius—
to stay beauty awhile, and keep her face.
Exegi monumentum aere perennius—
a poet at the foot of Pushkin's bronze.

Dear Michael (12)

I could say more about the victory
so much more, so very much more, until
saying the word *sun* is to speak of it
the shining victory in the face of day
that is the nature of semantics, I mean
that is the profit of excess, to see
one throw of dice co-author a page
you learned by heart, in a no-man's-land
the barbed-wire compound called a city
on the eve of combat. The scribe liked
icon dragons and golden leafy capitals.
He was the last scribe, the last page
was his to complete, on the final day
of the last city that was left to him.
You see the logic of his position?
Euclid's theses of imaginary surfaces
point without size, line and area
obedient to pure reason, and perfect cubes
reflecting peerless hyperbolas—
it pleased him to recite such marvels
writing the last law on the last quarto
the last pen moving in the last hand.
The final scribe in the only library
the only river roaring in the forest
are equivalent, and in truth one may say
that the last cricket at the last harvest
describes the same pathos, the last
become the first, the first to be last
the only sun gleaming in the only weather
the only scribe to sit alone in a city
to write the only cursive, primordial
characters of the sole intelligence.
Others agree that it was always thus
—the victor eliminates the victim—
this is the world that thought built.

Dear Michael (13)

There is a way of thinking, of being
involved across the counter of a
Chinese shop, with the smell of cod fish
watering the eyes, and burlap sacks.
And thus begins an exchange of senses
eye for touch, and ear for ear-of-corn
fractal thought as in a net of nouns
finding a near mis(take) chicken backs
cow tongue and a dish heaped with fudge—
recalling a subject inside the shop
buying and looking at tins of sardines.
Involved with shillings when young.
Involved with value, or as some reckon
the cartouche with Hannibal's face
with elephant on the obverse, crossing
the steep ravines among his foot soldiers.
(Making do *with* is the point. Migrant
throngs pour through this difference.)
I could say more about the old mill
sluicing water and flagstones and moss
on three sides of the courtyard.
I could bark an order to the housemaid:
tell the tinker to fetch in the pots.
And if the milk-man comes on his wagon
the broom-man on his bicycle, then fetch in
broom and milk and also give an ear to
the peanut-man's whistle, the post-man's
bell, the icicle-man's shout, the gas-
company man, the electric inspector
come to inspect the wiring and switch.
I could say more about the birds-of-paradise.
Look, here they bloom in a photo from 1912.
The distance you feel is the ground
of understanding grown thin and weathered
a ligature blown dry and unapparent.

Dear Michael (14)

The tongue is a dry leaf that drifts
mimetic from steeple to bougainvillea
echo and name-giver and once a toll
exacted from immigrants, other-speakers
trailing tales through the arable yard
to entrepôt of zero-orchid, null-nectar
cisterns, ghettos and broken taxis
and ventilators broken, in an arid house.
Imagine a peacock fronting the Age of Botany.
A rhapsode sits singing in the house.
Imagine a language, ligature and plume.
He sings of piston and pistil, air wave
and lyric theory, the chain of magnets
arcing from flower to tholepin, scrape
of echoes in an airshaft—troubled sleep.
Scar of glass and weed in a vacant lot
the tin cans and leaky pipes, episode
patterned on the sun's angle restored
to its major chord. I hear footsteps.
Air circles the footsteps of a peacock.
Imagine a language, ligature and plume.
Beyond the edge where language falters
only air circles the Pantheon, built from
thunder, local to oral, and sunlight—
anemone, and the plasma of mud—
souvenirs of the wreck and metaphors
to fix passage at the core of the day
the nation we leave, and take along.

Three Aspects of the Name

1. The Stencil of My Device

At the threshold of morning I encountered a ghost, my name.
We quarreled, because I was of a more venerable caste
than what the name announced, a violent clan of laborers,
men given to dance in the costume of underworld spirits
who took ship with the merchants from the Gold Coast, and blew
ashore in the Latitudes of Weeping. Skilled at the machete
we cut down trees to fashion a secret bivouac in the hills.
The regiment came, flying the colors, to scatter and perish.
As time went on the news of these battles wore away
like earth from constant rainfall. We went from the hills
to settle the fertile lands about the capital. My ancestors
bore sons and daughters to men who reached the plantation
by other routes, and with other prospects. Hence the stencil
of my device, invisible to mirrors, but still vocal
like the echo of grief, which we alone perceive, detached
from the body though not replaced. The name remembers
events best left to the whistle of tree frogs at night.
A scent of orchids disguises the past, whereas the name
like a breeze in the pines infiltrates the landscape
and causes discomfort. Crickets whir in the midnight grass.

The gospel tells us that tradition flows like a river
to irrigate the soul, from origin to the fringe
of reason. It is the thing you can't avoid belonging to
just as the sea cannot escape mingling with water.
The voice of tradition is ours, or else we are empty
forms cast aside like husks from a coconut grove
able to lie in the sun but not to speak of the havoc
of hunger, or so the philosophers aver, in their moods.
The history of the tribe is fixed within the orbit
traced by the name in written records. Nothing else exists.

11. The Stream at Mavis Bank

The stream at Mavis Bank overflows the roadway.
The place is forever tinted in sunlight—
the water slipping around boulders, twisting
flows dipping and boiling over with froth.
To bathe in this stream is a rite of passage.
Deep or shallow, the water saturates the name
fetched from the city, together with the language
that cradles its previous owners, the planters
in high boots wading through guinea grass
toward a mill house, stolid in the morning dew.

On the island, nothing is hidden; every surface
contains the whole of the pattern, like a fractal
shape reproducing an arabesque of error
sutured to integral gesture, the confident practice
of place. The river escapes from this pattern.
The water flows without warning, into the middle
of a road, to supplant the archival voice.
No scribe has planted the river into memory.
Cold water on the skin at dawn is the only naming.

iii. The Dominion of Grammaticus

The river is always flowing, always there
it fills the stanza of the dithyramb
with forces and driftwood and cadence.
It unites here with the wild. It connects
seaport to inland sea to urban oasis
of unsuitable livery, worn at the sleeve.

.   .   .   .

To believe that a name fits you badly
like a suit of creaky armor, or the name
turns prism into prison, and filters light
as interference pattern, surely it is
that this purpose is given in the nature
of signs, which drop from above. For the name
belongs to the dominion of Grammaticus.

.   .   .   .

The epic narrative, rolling forward,
soon discovers an old man kneeling
to kiss the hands that took the life
of his son. That's what it says
plain as snowy Atlas and Olympus.
Camped by the sea, the alien tribe
is my force, my people. The scout leaning
at the cave door watches the way
to the mountain bivouac, where song
is forbidden. No epic tradition records
this passage to liberty of the dead.

Letters to Michael

Dear Michael (15)

If to speak, then one must
perforce decide
since it is not enough
to want a thing, to open
the heart to read
therein the letters
Accompong   St. Elizabeth
other punctual vectors
that run   changeable
daring   particular
and which for all that
the body knows were
there at the beginning, to be
copied just so, like this
the stroke of a pen
doubling what the mind
says to itself, to others,
and yet for the first time
able to speak unbidden
by those that are the sins
of vanity, worthy
of death, sitting still
at a candle—I say no
one must decide
therewithal to forget
the heart, its song
the lips of memory
you kissed once in the dark
apse where bells boomed
melancholy hymns.

Dear Michael (16)

I was looking for a book that no one had read
a starlight treatise, the lost book
the book without an author that the Vikings
forgot in their drunkenness, since to write
a book one must read the pages by candle.
Knowledge enters the world. The book is a door
but the unread text has no features to copy
and has no hand to tease the paleographer
out of himself, sick of chants, buried
alive in a dismal century. The readerless book
imagines a world before the alphabet. It is
immune to exegesis, and therefore beloved
and promises to speak the truth like a desert.
Pilgrims go to visit the locale. It is said
that they do. It is said that they live
among us in the days of forgetting, the absent
readers of a delicate codex unknown to time
but forecast, swaddled in emerald cladding.
Under the blink of stars, the book lies open.
The arms of the book invite the lover
to stay for a while in the curve of final thought
to travel without moving through gardens
to a dry place that has no symbol or agenda.

In a city behind the fog, where the Barbarian
long ago was king, only shadows stir today.
Innkeepers, engineers, and bureaucrats of the state
slipped into exile, or met the night
like wind in trees at the edge of a garrison.
The long night is longer without the throng.

Dear Michael (17)

I remember the talk when you said Rodchenko
had taught you things, and today I saw
a man on a tower with an aeroplane nearby
and a crowd, and a woman with a large mouth
who was the future, white buildings that curve
like the street curves in London, February
in a metropolis. Technique passes. Photo-
montage signals happiness and redeems
nothing more than ice cream, it's just art
just a change from the hotel-room wallpaper—
brown-beige, greasy, indestructible—
Mayakovsky's rectangular head in triplicate
workers at the White Sea Canal—200,000 dead—
and utopia on everyone's to-do list. Privately,
I detest culture, think of postcolonial
as a silhouette missing its interior organs
a hulking shape like history airbrushed
from a photograph you glance at to confirm:
I was once here looking at the empty landscape
of Paris's banlieue, on a Sunday afternoon,
down among the concrete walkways, and no one
hailed me from a window or a bicycle seat.
And then I went to the city, and other events
assembled like a heap of whiskey bottles
someone got lost in, a labyrinth of glass.
One day I went to see Rodchenko's photographs
at a London exhibition, finally. I'm still waiting,
like everyone else, for the magic thunderclap.
But perhaps you meant the painting and sculpture
which he abandoned for the camera, in the 1920s.

The Physics of Identity in Late Age

At twilight, the music is faint. At night, it is
as if it never was, the dithyramb. Bereft, I tried
to empty my head of all but the essential things.
My model was Villon, who left the daylight happy
to bequeath abundant curses to his friends. I made
a list of tropical flowers and a separate table
of the contents of lists and of the mercenary plants
that we saw in Cappadocia on the final march.
Time was then, now, and later, and I was out of sorts,
creeping up to the bedroom window of the old house
to see the beginning of the downfall and the way
the membrane fractured, and I went to redshift
knowing pieces only of the island that is the soul's
connection to syllables. Each one must tend to
his own plot of the earth. But I was a microdot,
an ant, a drift of foam, scarcely more than orchid
son of an imaginary number, so that I might sing
this poem about nothing is the flower of my genesis.
As it was, so it is, and will be, for this one and all.
The song of the rain I heard when I was a boy
still falls imperceptibly on zinc roof
on tile, on wood, on glass, on leaf, on string.

A man lives over there in a gully. They say he is mad.
He walks the roads naked; he has hair like a bush.
The sun explodes and devours the law of gravity, and planets
orbit each other in a Niagara of rocks. This will happen,
and the rusty creak of legions or conquistadors
in armor will fatten the vortex. Restless music
of the coastal lands that saw the conquests begin
the tremble of mud. I was a vessel the wind used
to talk to the mast. The tempo of rain is my heirloom.

Artificial Songs

I.

What cannot be named does not exist.

To the oral and local bricoleur
devising signals from
broken statues to recommend
peace or battle, the river brings
all the needed vowels right
to his table, where he retrieves
useful things from the indistinct
shapes given to his compadres.

What can yet be named might not exist.

Of no use to him is the lexicon
ambient and plenary
plundered from the vault at Syracuse:
the perfected coincidence
of what to say and what is real
the noise of an ambush
that comes or will come to pass
watches over his labors.

II.

The morning air fresh and lucid
and permeable to the resplendent city
sunlight radiates to the white
corner of the bedroom, and the two
of us inside the visible
spaces alive with glory
the writing desk, floor lamp, and shelf.

The name sings. The name does not lie.

The room, tethered, fills up
with air fills up with floating sun
timeless particles
the promise of articulate
artificial songs
the mud of last night's avalanche
banished from the transitory window.

The name sings. The name does not lie.

Passing between us is the name
thereafter unavailable once
the sun's angle widens
over the city and its river.
What the alphabet says it says
to no one save the rafter, penitential
man who rides the daylight.

The name sings. The name does not lie.

III.

The river flows calmly below.
The surface is brown, coated
in sunlight; an island
sits in the middle, green
bush covering earth and rocks.

I own to no name but my own.

The farther bank lies in shadow.
Each one of us is called ξ
the Proper Name, or Zero
or Bait-and-Switch, or Echo's
Orphan, history's essential guest.

I own to no name but my own.

Inescapable Country

Inside the world, the world is present.
It fills the mind with whistling
of birds, the golden flowers of pouis.

The ravines, along which scouts
pressed their enemies to a standstill,
throw up white blossoms of azaleas.

The paths are steep to the villages
splashed on the blue mountain ridges.
The cows in the pasture barely stir.

Something about pastoral calms
the violent heart, wherein desire
takes form in the visible world.

Bending a corner, you see it green
as it once was and will be then
and always with the mind's deceit.

Epitaphs

—Seen on a Tomb in a Remote Land—

If you should one day visit my homeland,
stranger, recall these details of my life
and bear to them that love me this message:

Here lies Melopoios. My father was libertinus.
I sang the love of women and the choral dance.
Cut down in battle, my soul fled to Hades.
Say then that I lost the sun too cheaply
fighting for a dead republic in another man's
country. But say also that I did not kneel.

<>

—Seen on a Tomb at Naqada, Near Thebes—

You who chance upon this tomb,
stranger, be of good cheer. For it is
time to sleep. The reign of Π
stretches to treeless infinity.

<>

—Seen on a Tomb in the Greater Antilles—

Hesitate, stranger, in your way, to bring word
from those who lie asleep before your feet:
We are the ones who did not die in the Passage.

<>

—Seen on a Tomb at Sunrise—

Portland was my nurse, and liberty
my obsession. Nameless, I fought the Regiment
at Trelawny Town. Depart now, stranger,
from this tomb under the withered
magnolia. There is nothing you can do for me.

<>

—Seen on a Deserted Coast—

Stranger, my story is brief. The captain
landed me here, in mist and salt wind.
I fought and fell, and went down to Styx.

<>

—Seen on a Tomb at the Crossroads—

Old age has conquered my limbs. My eyes fail.
Repeat this caution, stranger, to anyone
yet hale, that he might plan a better verse.

<>

—Seen on a Tomb in a Frontispiece—

The vintage cup was my altar
the grapevine my cathedral.
Blessed, as a youth I sang
conquest, revolt, migration
to Romans, slaves, exiles.
In time, I became non grata.
Elderly, I went from the city
to alien constellations
to alien forests and rivers
among the pale barbarians.
Stranger, I bid you tarry
here, at this neglected tomb,
to read these words aloud
from my heart, and for my sake.

Dear K

(Not of the republic is this the day of beginning.)

And if it is not yet spoken, this day, what it is
if I cannot speak about it, to you, my love,
to anyone, of the picture, time of here
and time to come, how long the beginning
the after of any season, how to count on it
I do not know. The poem inclines
to restless thought: the night relentless
the heavens unimaginably vast. I cannot speak
of else that troubles me but that this
appears, needs to be worded, to you, to someone
but to you above all, the sky in January
crowded with lights, we saw them, on our back
on a deck, and the sea nearby, flowing and going.

—APRIL 10, 2004

COLOPHON

Entrepôt was designed at Coffee House Press, in the historic
Grain Belt Brewery's Bottling House near downtown Minneapolis.
The text is set in Caslon.

FUNDER ACKNOWLEDGMENTS

Coffee House Press receives major operating support from the Bush Foundation, the McKnight Foundation, from Target, and from the Minnesota State Arts Board, through an appropriation from the Minnesota State Legislature and from the National Endowment for the Arts, a federal agency. Coffee House also receives support from: three anonymous donors; Abraham Associates; the Elmer L. and Eleanor J. Andersen Foundation; Allan Appel; Around Town Literary Media Guides; Bill Berkson; the James L. and Nancy J. Bildner Foundation; the Patrick and Aimee Butler Family Foundation; the Buuck Family Foundation; Dorsey & Whitney, LLP; Fredrikson & Byron, P.A.; Jennifer Haugh; Anselm Hollo and Jane Dalrymple-Hollo; Jeffrey Hom; Stephen and Isabel Keating; Robert and Margaret Kinney; the Kenneth Koch Literary Estate; Allan & Cinda Kornblum; the Lenfestey Family Foundation; Ethan J. Litman; Mary McDermid; Rebecca Rand; Debby Reynolds; Schwegman, Lundberg, Woessner, P.A.; Charles Steffey and Suzannah Martin; John Sjoberg; Jeffrey Sugerman; Stu Wilson and Mel Barker; the Archie D. & Bertha H. Walker Foundation; the Woessner Freeman Family Foundation in memory of David Hilton; and many other generous individual donors.

This activity is made possible in part by a grant from the Minnesota State Arts Board, through an appropriation by the Minnesota State Legislature and a grant from the National Endowment for the Arts. MINNESOTA STATE ARTS BOARD

TARGET.

To you and our many readers across the country,
we send our thanks for your continuing support.

Good books are brewing at www.coffeehousepress.org